JUNIOR BIOS

Idina Menzel

BY KRISTEN RAJCZAK NELSON

Enslow PUBLISHING

Please visit our website, www.enslow.com. For a free color catalog of all our high-quality books, call toll free 1-800-398-2504 or fax 1-877-980-4454.

Library of Congress Cataloging-in-Publication Data
Names: Rajczak Nelson, Kristen, author.
Title: Idina Menzel / Kristen Rajczak Nelson.
Description: New York : Enslow Publishing, [2022] | Series: Junior bios | Includes index.
Identifiers: LCCN 2020036893 (print) | LCCN 2020036894 (ebook) | ISBN 9781978525320 (library binding) | ISBN 9781978525306 (paperback) | ISBN 9781978525313 (set) | ISBN 9781978525337 (ebook)
Subjects: LCSH: Menzel, Idina–Juvenile literature. | Singers–United States–Biography–Juvenile literature. | Actors–United States–Biography–Juvenile literature.
Classification: LCC ML420.M3825 R35 2022 (print) | LCC ML420.M3825 (ebook) | DDC 782.42164092 [B]–dc23
LC record available at https://lccn.loc.gov/2020036893
LC ebook record available at https://lccn.loc.gov/2020036894

First Edition

Published in 2022 by
Enslow Publishing
29 E. 21st Street
New York, NY 10010

Designer: Deanna Paternostro
Editor: Kate Mikoley

Photo credits: Cover, p. 1 (Idina Menzel) Feature5ash Photo Agency/Shutterstock.com; cover, p. 1 (photo frame) Aleksandr Andrushkiv/Shutterstock.com; marble texture used throughout HardtIllustrations/Shutterstock.com; lined paper texture used throughout Mtsaride/Shutterstock.com; watercolor texture used throughout solarbird/Shutterstock.com; p. 5 Albert L. Ortega/Contributor/Getty Images Entertainment/Getty Images; p. 7 Time & Life Pictures/Contributor/The LIFE Picture Collection/Getty Images; p. 9 Bruce Glikas/Contributor/FilmMagic/Getty Images; p. 11 Frank Micelotta/Staff/Getty Images Entertainment/Getty Images; p. 13 E. Charbonneau/Staff/WireImage/Getty Images; p. 15 Drew Angerer/Stringer/Getty Images News/Getty Images; p. 17 Robert Gauthier/Contributor/Los Angeles Times/Getty Images; p. 17 (inset) Alberto E. Rodriguez/Staff/Getty Images Entertainment/Getty Images; p. 19 Focus On Sport/Contributor/Getty Images Sport/Getty Images.

Printed in the United States of America

CPSIA compliance information: Batch #CWENS22: For further information contact Enslow Publishing, New York, New York, at 1-800-398-2504.

Contents

Words in the glossary appear in **bold** type the first time they are used in the text.

An Iconic Voice

From "Defying Gravity" to "Into the Unknown," Idina Menzel has powerfully voiced some of the most **iconic** songs in recent memory. But when Idina was young, she hid her talent and didn't want to be known as a show-off.

Still, she can't remember a time when she didn't want to perform. Idina was born in New York City on May 30, 1971, and started singing and acting as a child. Idina went to college at the famous New York University Tisch School of the Arts.

IDINA IS THE FIRST TO POINT OUT THAT THE BIG HIGHS OF HER **CAREER** HAVE BEEN MANY YEARS APART. SHE TOLD *VARIETY*: "HAVING A CAREER THAT GOES UP AND DOWN HAS MADE ME REALLY [VALUE] WHEN I DO HAVE SUCCESS."

FACTS BEHIND THE FIGURE

By age 15, Idina was singing at weddings on the weekends to make money.

Everything Starts with *Rent*

Idina's first theater job after college was in the musical *Rent*. The show started Off-Broadway and quickly moved to Broadway, opening April 29, 1996. Idina played Maureen Johnson, a part that needed a singer with a big voice. The show was a huge hit!

FACTS BEHIND THE FIGURE

Idina returned to Broadway in September 2001 as Amneris in the musical *Aida*.

RENT PUT IDINA IN THE SPOTLIGHT FOR THE FIRST TIME.

For her **role** as Maureen, Idina got her first Tony Award **nomination** for Best Performance by a Featured Actress in a Musical. Though she didn't win, *Rent* won four other Tonys, including Best Musical.

Going Green

Following her success in *Rent*, Idina recorded two albums, one in 1998 and one in 2002. Neither sold very well. Then, she had another big break—and it was back to Broadway.

In Her Own Words

"For me, Rent was all about coming out of myself, finding out who I was, learning the power I could have as a performer. And Wicked was about harnessing all that strength."

IDINA STARRED IN *WICKED* ALONGSIDE KRISTIN CHENOWETH AS GLINDA.

In 2003, Idina **originated** the role of the Wicked Witch of the West, Elphaba, in the Broadway musical *Wicked*. Costumes and makeup made her green every night, but nothing could cover her famous voice on the showstopping numbers "The Wizard and I," "Defying Gravity," and "No Good Deed."

Audiences were wowed by Idina's performance as Elphaba. Her work was a large part of why *Wicked* was such a huge success. It also earned her more award nominations, including a Tony Award nomination for Best Performance by a Leading Actress in a Musical. She won!

FACTS BEHIND THE FIGURE

Idina returned to the role of Maureen in *Rent* for the 2005 movie made of the musical.

IDINA PERFORMED "DEFYING GRAVITY" AT THE 2004 TONYS, THE NIGHT SHE WON HER TONY AWARD FOR WICKED.

Idina performed in the Broadway show until January 2005. She played Elphaba again in 2006 when *Wicked* opened in London, England. *Wicked* went on to become one of the highest-**grossing** Broadway musicals of all time.

Off-Broadway and On Screen

The next few years were busy for Idina, though not on Broadway. She starred in an Off-Broadway musical called *See What I Wanna See* in 2005. In 2007, she appeared in the Disney movie *Enchanted*.

Idina's son, Walker, was born in September 2009. It changed her as a performer: "My **expectations** of myself are lower because I can only be in so many places at one time. So, when I get on stage, I feel [freed] and easier on myself, and therefore, I'm actually better."

ENCHANTED WAS A MUSICAL MOVIE STARRING AMY ADAMS, BUT IDINA DOESN'T SING IN IT!

The year 2010 brought even more success for Idina. She began appearing on the musical TV show *Glee*. She also performed at the White House for President Barack Obama and First Lady Michelle Obama!

That year, she also helped found A BroaderWay. Among other programs, the **foundation** set up a summer camp where girls could learn about performing, making art, and building community. "It's about using the arts to help girls find their own voice," Idina said of the foundation.

IDINA SANG AT THE WHITE HOUSE AGAIN AT THE 2016 EASTER EGG ROLL.

Letting It All Go

Idina has called the successes of her career "lightning in a bottle." It struck again in 2013 when Idina voiced Elsa in the Disney movie *Frozen*. It made Idina part of one of the highest-grossing **animated** movies of all time. She also scored a hit song with "Let It Go," which showed off Idina's strong voice as well as an **inspirational** message.

In Her Own Words

"I love to sing ["Let It Go."]... that makes me really proud—that I have that in my career, that I have a song and a character and a movie that is so powerful and really changes people."

WITH "LET IT GO," IDINA BECAME THE FIRST PERSON TO EVER HAVE A BILLBOARD TOP 10 HIT SONG AS WELL AS A TONY AWARD FOR ACTING!

"Let It Go" won the Academy Award for Best Original Song at the 2014 Oscars. Idina performed the song at the show!

Back to Broadway

In 2014, Idina headed back to Broadway to star in *If/Then*. The part was written with her in mind, and she was on stage for nearly the whole show. Idina's hard work paid off. She was again nominated for a Tony Award for Best Performance by a Leading Actress in a Musical. While she didn't win, it showed Idina still could rule a Broadway stage.

FACTS BEHIND THE FIGURE

In late 2014, Idina put out her first Christmas album, *Holiday Wishes*. It reached the top 10 on the *Billboard* Top 200 Albums chart!

MILLIONS OF PEOPLE WATCHED IDINA SING THE NATIONAL ANTHEM AT THE SUPER BOWL.

Idina conquered another big stage in 2015: the Super Bowl! Idina sang the national anthem before Super Bowl XLIX in Arizona.

Reaching Higher

Idina returned to the big screen in 2019 as Elsa in *Frozen 2*. The movie again showcased Idina's gravity-defying voice with "Into the Unknown" and "Show Yourself." The movie made $1.2 billion worldwide and continued Idina's rise as a true superstar. In fact, in 2019, both she and costar Kristen Bell received stars on the Hollywood Walk of Fame!

From Elphaba to Elsa, Idina's roles have brought her success nearly unmatched by another performer. What more will she accomplish?

FACTS BEHIND THE FIGURE

Idina has performed around the world, singing songs from her many albums and the shows and movies she's been a part of.

Idina's Timeline

1971: IDINA IS BORN ON MAY 30.

1996: *RENT* OPENS ON BROADWAY.
IDINA IS NOMINATED FOR A TONY AWARD.

1998: IDINA PUTS OUT HER FIRST ALBUM.

2001: SHE PERFORMS IN *AIDA* ON BROADWAY.

2003: *WICKED* OPENS ON BROADWAY.

2004: IDINA WINS A TONY AWARD FOR HER ROLE AS ELPHABA IN *WICKED*.

2009: HER SON, WALKER, IS BORN.

2010: IDINA BEGINS APPEARING ON *GLEE*.
SHE PERFORMS AT THE WHITE HOUSE FOR THE FIRST TIME.

2013: *FROZEN* COMES OUT.

2014: *IF/THEN* OPENS ON BROADWAY.
IDINA IS NOMINATED FOR A TONY AWARD.

2015: IDINA SINGS THE NATIONAL ANTHEM AT THE SUPER BOWL.

2019: *FROZEN 2* COMES OUT.
IDINA RECEIVES A STAR ON THE HOLLYWOOD WALK OF FAME.

Glossary

animated Consisting of drawings or computer images that appear to move.

career The job someone chooses to do for a long time.

expectation A belief that something is likely to happen.

foundation A not-for-profit organization provided with funds to support charitable works.

gross To earn an amount of money.

iconic Having to do with something very successful or admired.

inspirational Causing people to want to do something.

nomination An official suggestion for an honor. To nominate is to officially suggest for an honor.

originate To be the first to play a part.

role A part a person plays.

For More Information

Books

Allman, John Robert. *A Is for Audra: Broadway's Leading Ladies from A to Z*. New York, NY: Doubleday Books for Young Readers, 2019.

Schumacher, Thomas. *How Does the Show Go On? The Frozen Edition: An Introduction to the Theater*. Glendale, CA: Disney Editions, 2019.

Websites

Idina Menzel
idinamenzel.com/
Keep up with Idina Menzel on her website.

Idina Menzel Biography
www.broadway.com/buzz/stars/idina-menzel/profile/
Find the latest videos and information about Idina Menzel here.

Publisher's note to educators and parents: Our editors have carefully reviewed these websites to ensure that they are suitable for students. Many websites change frequently, however, and we cannot guarantee that a site's future contents will continue to meet our high standards of quality and educational value. Be advised that students should be closely supervised whenever they access the internet.

Index